The Skáld and the Drukkin Tröllaukin:
Photographs and Poems of Iceland

Paul Brooke

ISBN 978-1-7377808-1-6
Copyright © 2022 Paul Brooke
Published by Gold Wake Press
Cover Design by Paul Brooke
Book Interior by Paul Brooke
No part of this book may be reproduced except in brief quotations and in reviews without permission from the publisher.
The Skáld and the Drukkin Trollaukin
Published 2022, Paul Brooke
goldwake.com

The Skald and the Drukkin Trollaukin:
Photographs and Poems of Iceland

Table of Contents

Poems:

Rindhendur (Poem by Snorri Sturlson)	7
The Shore of Corpses	8
Urriðafoss	10
Invisible Giants	15
The Skáld and the Dóttir of Cairn	16
Tolerance to Arsenic	24
Leaf-Isle	27
The Kind Mink	28
Kakistocracy	30
Aftermath	32
The Landscape	35
Haifoss	36
The Skáld and the Drukkin Tröllaukin	39
The Mead of Poetry	50
Kerið Crater	52
Six Angles of Puffins	56
Vermin	60
Svartifoss	62
Myths and Rumors	64
Reversal of Misfortune	67
Smoldering	68
Visible Giants	71
The Shore of Corpses II	72
Notes on Poems	74
Works Cited	76

Photographs:

Skógafoss	5
Black-Tailed Godwit	6
Reynisdranger	8-9
Urriðafoss Waterfall and Fisherman	10
Icelandic Horse	12-13
Reynisdranger Tröll Rock	14
Black and White Glacial Ice at Jökulsárlon	17
Stone Man	23
Tombstone	25
BW Infrared Moss at Thingvallir	26
Mink	29
Black and White Infrared Rapids	31
Black and White Svartifoss	32-33
Jökulsárlón Glacial Lagoon Ice	34
Haifoss Waterfall	36-37
Tröll Sheep Barn	38
Buðir Church in Snaesfellsnes	41
Turf House	42
Oystercatcher on Nest	46-47
Oystercatcher Eggs	48-49
Common Murre Egg	53
Kerið Crater	53-55
Atlantic Puffins	57-59
Blue Arctic Fox with Puffin Kill	61
Svartifoss	63
Drangslið II Beneath Eyjafjöll Mountains	64-65
Spring Waterfall	66
Gardar, Beached Whaling Ship	69
Skogafoss in Infrared	70
Lupine	73
King Eider Chick	75

Ridhendur

Él threifsk skarpt of Skúla
skys snarvinda lindar,
egg vard hvöss höggum
hraes dynbrunnum runnin.
Sveimthreytir bió sveita
sniallr ilstafna hrafni.
Páll vard und fet falla
fram thrábarni arnar.

The sharp storm of the keen
spear-wind cloud raged around Skuli,
the sharp edge was flooded
with rushing corpse-streams amid the blows.
The brave turmoil-performer covered
the raven's claws with blood.
Paul had to fall down beneath
the treat of the eagle's beloved offspring.

—Sturluson 1987

The Shore of Corpses
—a Ljoðahattr, an ancient Norse form

In Corpse-Strand Hall, land-murderers
and oath-breakers waded in inky rivers
of poison. Blue serpents were cross-
stitched into the roof. Fangs faced down
oozing venom. The bane of rain burned
and scalded, killing the kind-hearted.

The Hall's dismal laws demolished rock
and knocked apart the earth. Goodness
blocked. Hooks became trawling nets.
Knives became greedy engines. Glaciers
calved countries. People were chained
to being only what they were told to be.

Slicked-backed cetaceans laid inert;
their corpses reached to infinitude
along the beach. Their black bodies
languished on black sand, darkness
eclipsing, overtaking them. The moon
and sun swallowed by Skoll and Hati.

Stars smothered, withered from sight.
Summer extinguished. Evil mounted.
Fights catapulted. Final brutal winter.
Humankind mired in lies and incest,
made mad by iniquity. The earth tired,
burned out and ready for a revolution.

The flaming sons of the world poured
forth to purge the newest bacteria,
the strain, the drain to future's hope:
humans. Rotten mountains imploded
from inside out, while lava slurped
in spasmodic burps and scoured land.

Scorched and torched, all grass burned.
Possessions dropped. Parents schlepped
children. Children clung to parents. People
wept as they scurried to the cliff to escape
the doomsday of the gods. We all lined up
along the edge, cloistered and cornered.

Urriðafoss

I magically survive the onslaught:
impassable roads, treeless winds,

ice crystals pelting the glass, a bent
rim, and a broken tire iron and finger.

An old woman ridicules me driving
in this mess. The safe bet is home,

make no hasty decisions, never
disrupt others, never destroy

children's lives, never risk anything
for an alternative vision. Stay true.

Don't veer. The roads here do not
forgive. I feel sealed in a Norse myth,

A woman moans her husband's loss.
A man groans out his lovesickness

and inhabits perpetual doom. Echoed
in wind, I hear their pain and understand.

Despite suffering for years, I feel
released, internalize this mountain,

swallow it like a communion wafer
and let it dissolve and disseminate

through my body. It rises each night
in my eyes and retreats each morning

like an enormous ice berg, calved,
casually drifting in the Greenland Sea.

Eventually, all things melt, mesh
and join like freshet and briny.

Eventually, all things disintegrate
and mix like jouissance and hate.

Eventually, the horses will return
from the mountains after the blizzard.

Within this estuary and embouchure,
no one stirs. As I trace my way along

the river, the lenticular clouds cap
the mountain, contrast the black rock

and new tufts of grass. I am here
in this confluence, in this pulsating

surge, foothold firm, relieved I risked
it all, proud I withstood all the threats,

faced the myths, the character
assassinations, the antagonist as hero.

Invisible Giants

"Einangrun dregur bunglyndi oft á langinn."

I am struggling under the skull sky,
trying to identify what I see and feel.
They are not frost-ogres but veritable
loners, invisible giants are trailing me.

In the Southwest, Einangrast bathes
in the glacial rivers and golden waterfalls.
Only I see his form backlit from droplets
of mist and water, sixteen meters in height.

In the West, Úr is a vigilante, exiled sentry
over pufflings. He stands back of the cliffs
and herds the confused new ones into the sea.
Even though they try to comply, some fail.

In the Northeast, Bömmer loves Sorg
but they are separated by curses and rivers.
He sleeps in a depression in the stone
forest, rocks echoing a melancholy melody.

In the East, Sorg weeps in the only treed
forest; she has forgotten touch and her lover's
voice. I realize the shallowness of my own
hurt in her sorrow. No certainty of tomorrow.

The Skáld and his Dottir of Cairn
—told through 22 hattatals, ancient Norse forms

Fornyrðislag
—Old Story Meter

Hag hid a gorcrow,
her son, in hay mow.
Skáld swung the scythe,
thoughtlessly, idly.
Never saw wrath,
no dire warning, death.
Skáld tightened at sight,
twilight of the Gods.

Liódaháttr
—Song Form

The stout always,
always slays the mouse-
shrew; it's all he ever knew.

The hag always,
always harangues through curse,
taking the pulse of her.

Málahattr
—Speech Form

"Skáld, you've slain my second
son with your worn out scythe;
I'm frost-mist, thin rime,
a frayed knot, a clay house.
I will turn one you love
into a stone tower,
a cairn, so you must decide,
your child or your bride?"

Idurmælt
—Repeatedly Said Verse

"Choosing is a losing win,
bruising abuse, doubled.
The killing never willing,
Branding me the villain.
The killing never willing,
deviling loved women.
Release me, cease,
seek peace, call a truce."

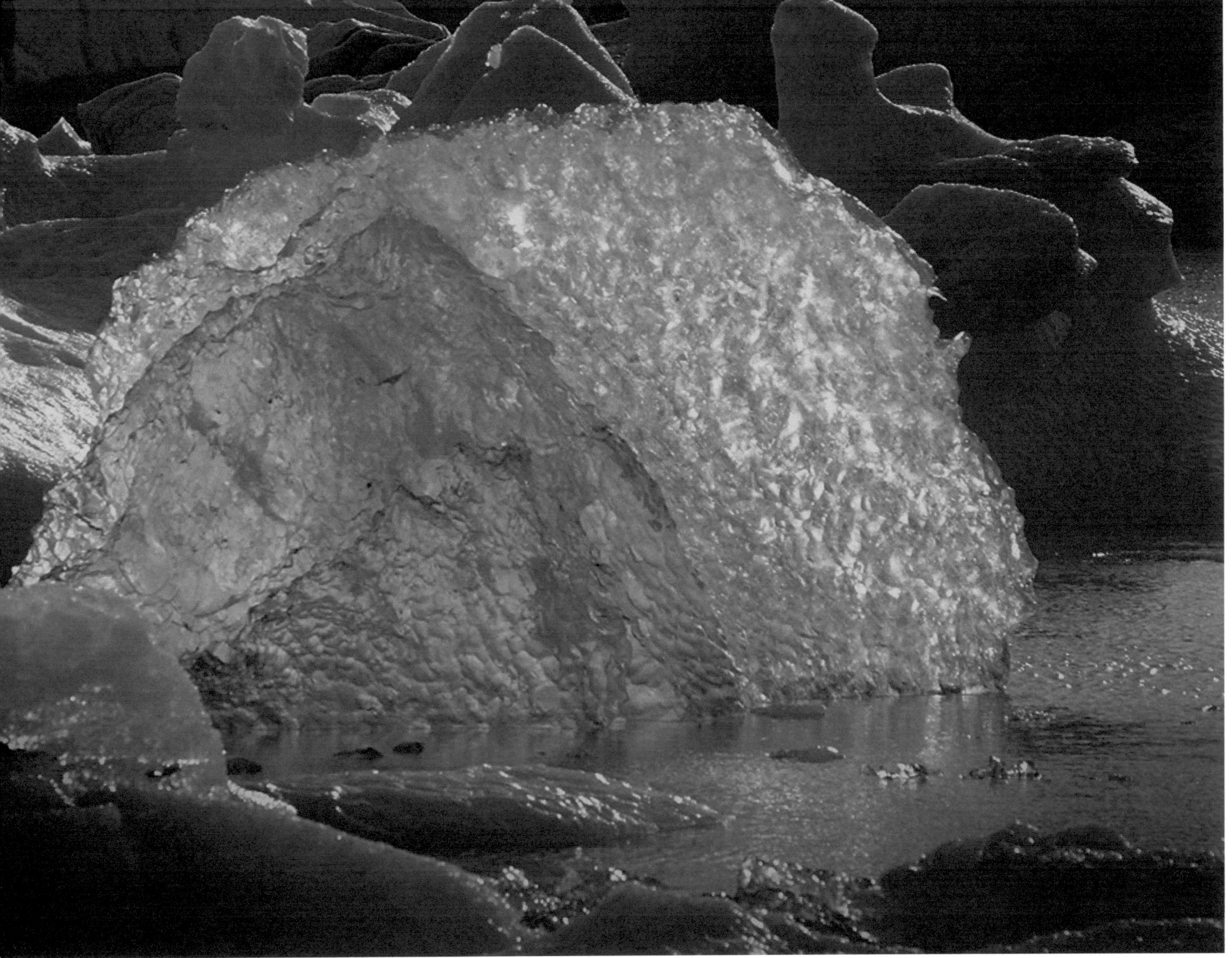

Klifat
—Repeated Verse

"No truce, Skáld, no excuse.
Noose tightens. Don't mischoose.
Can't recuse. Can't refuse.
You must choose. You must choose."
The skáld, looked appalled,
stalled, begging on knees, crawling,
wailing and bawling,
wailing and bawling.

Stúfar
—Docked Verse

"Stö∂va, don't use untruth, be
uncouth, overdramatic.
You know I'm your soothsayer,
youth taker, wish granter.
Your dóttir shall be saved
slaughter, held in stone.
She shall be released,
spared if you complete three."

Tilsagt
—Annotated Verse

"Plant a pine for each memory,
pleasant—pleasing memories—only.
Write seven poems each week,
wistful—metaphorical odes—only.
Unmelt glaciers, undo dams,
Unjam—the laxganga—the salmon.
Let them river flourish, find
flight—redd nourished—free."

Kimblabönd
—Bundle-Bond Verse

Skáld deflated, slunk away,
scolded, punished and afraid.
How could he complete
his three, unlock the cairn-key?
Fickle-minded, he fumbled
frantically for answers.
Undo dams, unmelt glaciers,
Unjam the flight of salmon?

Stúfhent
—*Stump-Rhymed Verse*

Laikskáld languished,
largely vanquished.
Wife held him well,
wisely, tears quelled.
Opt for one pine,
one tree a time.
Pen poems daily;
ply policy.

Nahent
—*Close-Rhyme Verse*

Spared, dust settled.
Sótop blocked, stopped.
Old dreadnought dropped;
distressed thoughts, boycott.
Left on his quest,
hopeful, coping. Sun-
graced glaciers held
greatness, spoiling hate.

Veggiat
—*Wedged Verse*

Thoughts turned, described, inscribed;
Tonnes of red fir seedlings bedded.
Skáld planted, penned, proved, planned,
(&) sat in dens with councilmen.
Honored his stone dóttir, nightly,
home, he read her poems, sweetly.
Like cloudlets shrouding light,
like slick rain on windowpanes.

Hagmælt
—*Skillfully Spoken Verse*

"Our world wilts, diseased;
we can no longer breathe.
Ice fields run, retreat,
roast from summer's heat.
Actis spoils our soil,
stains Europe's entrails.
We must act, we must
mend health or face death."

Toglag
—*Journey-Meter Verse*

Skáld travelled whole world,
witness to unfitness.
Five years passed, ten passed,
pressed forty countries.
People planted firs,
poplars, larch, (&) arched birch.
Many millions rise;
micro forests grow lush.

Greppaminni
—*Poet's Reminder Verse*

Why doesn't my dóttir change?
Don't I deserve her love?
Why smite my years of work?
Why crush my weakened soul?
Why aren't glaciers wider?
Why don't dams weaken?
Why does the world unlisten?
Why don't you answer, hag?

Hnugghent
—*Deprived Verse*

Depressed, Skáld slunk home saddened,
stunned, angered, shunned;
heart was vellum, soul was samfell;
sálmurs howled, cried
foul; five hundred poems lay like
felled gravestones, gave
no choice but conflict, violence,
criminal whim.

Skothendr
—*Half-Rhymed Verse*

Evil wins, legal loses,
logic becomes toxic.
My advice is incite
incorrigible fools.
Uneducate, unread,
Unstudy (&) uninform.
Consume, assume all wrong,
all who don't think like you.

Samhent
—*Coincidentally-Rhymed Verse*

Boosted Semtex boxes,
bomb-making tools, fuses.
Won't survive sacrifice,
sever Sog River Dam.
Pyrrhic victory pits
plus v. false negative,
martyr v. tender tyrant,
traitor v. twice spy.

Tiltekit
—*Linked Verse*

Three dams blown to debris,
destroyed, made cratered voids,
no leads for devilish deeds;
deft culprit left a cairn,
a symbol, a riddle,
a break through, a hot clue;
detectives did not know,
did not know what to do.

Rétthent
—*Consistently-Rhymed Verse*

Tactic disputed. River rerouted,
recovered. Salmon hovered,
weeks later, laying roe,
lifted past the impasse.
Enthralled, Skáld spent three hours,
slowly observed their sweep,
scrub of stone, bodies rubbed,
soirees of glee captured.

Lidhendur
—*Helping Rhyme Verse*

Skáld's body of work was shoddy,
secretly, no key reforms.
Humankind stayed stoneblind,
so hellbent, status quo.
Unconcerned by senseless seas,
sky high drought, coral burnout,
beached dolphins, besieged rorquals,
bungled oil spills, smuggled birds.

Detthendr
 —*Falling Rhyme Verse*

He wept after his dóttir;
he washed her stones, murmured
his shamed goodbyes, surmised
steindur was her transfer
to great Valhöll, he hurled
himself to ground and found
instead of stones, some bones,
some hair, tail fins, fish skin.

Drögur
 —*Drawings Verse*

Skin leathered, orbs shriveled,
Skáld laid among billions
of cairns, clattered, scattered,
crushed to shards. Arms snapped.
Beard shifted to basaltic lava,
body grew weighty, fissured.
His tongue pronounced ash; tears
tasted like lichen and ruin.

Tolerance to Arsenic

Each morning like Mithridates, I ingest
a small dose of arsenic, figuring it is best

to build up tolerance then be murdered
by a dictator's orders or slandered

by his evil misdeeds. After all these years,
I am gut checked, stock strong and fear

nothing on my plate. I have sent the taster
away and wait alone to face my accusers.

They do not know to how to articulate
themselves without his mouth. Their hate

is rote response, mere truisms. Meanwhile,
their dictator parties all night in style

with cases of imported wine and brandy,
drunken orgies, whores and celebrities.

They only see him during the day, façade
erected, a marble statue fashioned into a god.

But away, he transmogrifies into a fraud,
a louse with a penchant for flesh, a flawed

loyalty to his peasants. Rumors drift back
to them, but they do not believe, they lack

validity. They believe only what they see
and no matter what I claim or say they flee

from the hard, cold candor. He is their author,
their paragon, their false idol, their megastar.

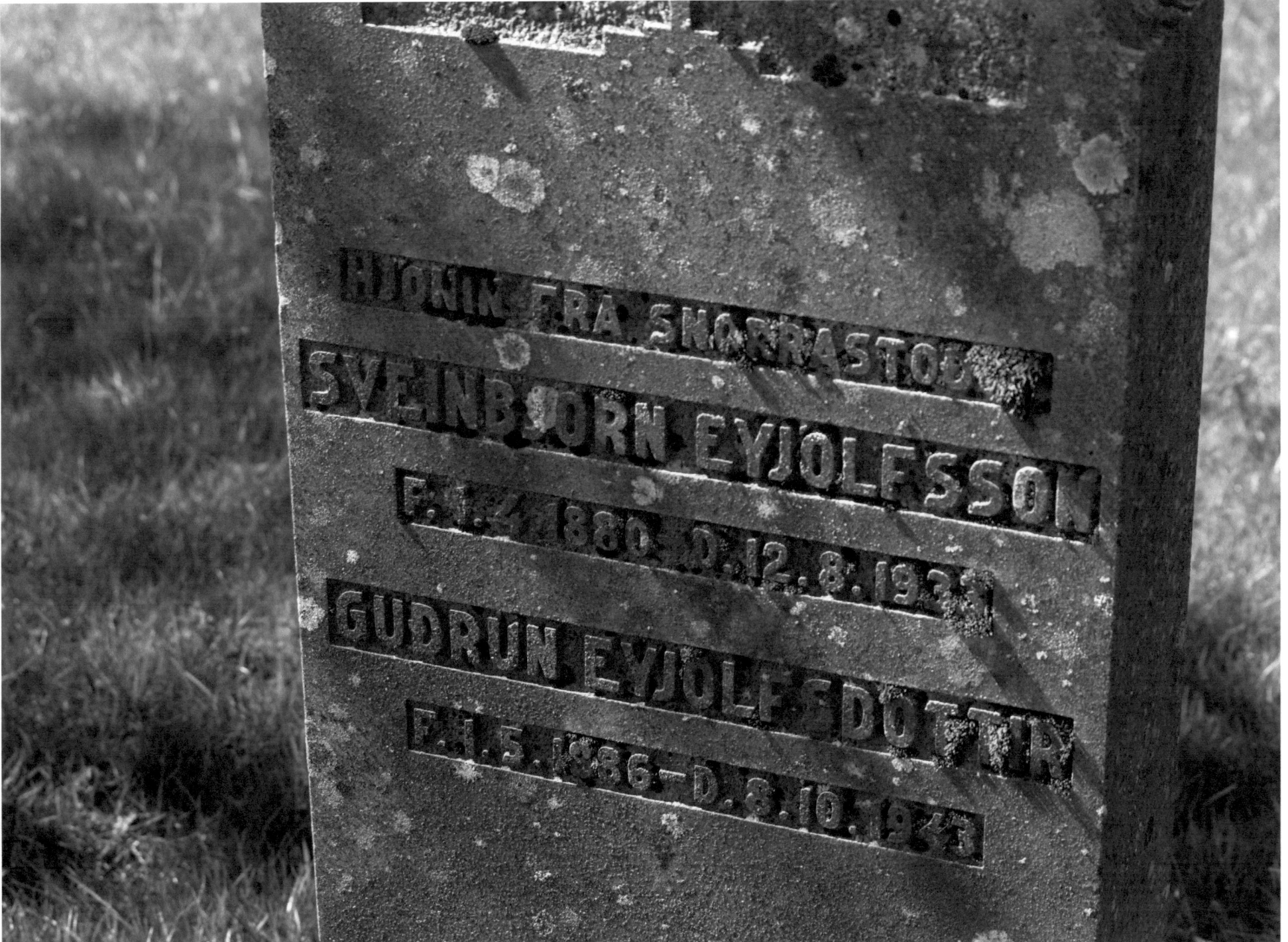

Leaf-Isle

*—a young man, who was like a son to me,
became involved in a cult and cut contact.*

He pretended the isle was pristine,
welcoming, no hint of bewitching.
There were tales of Farbauti's
hard-heartedness, but he conjured
Laufey, the beautiful one, instead.

There were caution signs to ponder,
counter to the scope and wonder.
The salt water was drinkable.
Wild boars will never kill you.
The agent seemed brutally honest.

He bought it and built a shifting
foundation on loose sand,
a dock with borrowed nails
and wormwood, and a chicken
coop with no locking door.

When friends and loved ones
said he was foolish, he rejected
them, spatting they were average,
mediocre, crushing and smashing
his dream, his vacation resort.

Soon, no one visited and he read
only books reinforcing his skew:
"Doubters will always exist. Do
not let them sway you. Tell them
there is only Plan A no Plan B."

His water supply was unusable.
A boar's tusk slit his leg to the bone.
Two foxes killed all his chickens.
His selling agent never answered him
so he figured she must be on vacation.

When he hallucinated and shook,
he tried to leave his isle but his motor
was pure gunk. His leg turned black
with gangrene. He was starving,
but he had to prove them wrong.

He applied a poison leaf to his leg,
wrapped it in book pages and husk,
boiled salt water over a fire, threw
a spear at a boar but missed and
then laid down never to stand again.

Two years later, his body ravaged
by boars, a caretaker buried his bones
in an unmarked grave and burned
the place to embers. At auction
in foreclosure, the skerry never sold.

The Kind-Mink
—a *Ljoðahattr*, an ancient Norse form

To rescue the kind water-mink,
I went up a rune, turned wide,
slid on my elbows, reached inside.
The den was waterlogged. Try
to wrangle one kit. Leave the evil other.
Remember defense is merely a posture.

I stretched, shoulder-deep in mud,
touched the first, waiting for a burst
of a blood, but nothing. On the right,
quietness and softness of fur,
an almost purr. I was blind and felt
his fat tummy, scratched behind his ear.

Halting, I thought of snatching him.
He must be the one, the kind-mink,
the fine-mink. This caused me pause.
I moved my hand across to the left,
felt fur, slightly damp, cramped,
curled in a tight little fist.

It bit me hard on the right wrist,
latched on like a leech, a nasty bugger,
tugging at my skin, numb at first,
then pinching pain. I pulled back,
panting, not knowing what to do.
Remember: defense is merely a posture!

What if the kind-mink was the mean-
mink? What if the mean feigned kind?
The side bled, not the front knuckles.
And the mean needed release.
I shifted my hand to the right
and no bite. In a split second, I decided.

I snagged the left-mink and pulled him
free. He was tiny, a little bib of white
under his chin, calm and cute,
chestnut brown, all wet fuzz
and whiskers. His eyes
were not petty nor pitiless.

The left-mink crawled up
my arm and laid across the back
of my neck like a miniature
scarf. His fur tickled;
he squeaked pleasantly
as if I was his mother.

The torment of years and fears,
unnecessary cruelty and tears,
turn of brother against brother,
disconnection to the daughter,
the reputation slaughter,
all the bad disappeared.

I knelt down and listened
deeply to the den. Inside,
the mean-mink was pissed,
hissed and shrieked. The kind-
mink climbed down into my jacket
pocket to sleep, peacefully.

We left evil behind, hiked
down, and found a brittle woman
in a bind. She laid sprawled
on the trail with a bad ankle sprain.
"My son had cancer and died.
He was supposed to be here."

She cried in spasms as I scooped
her up and carried her to the lot.
Slipping out of my pocket
into her lap, the kind-mink
calmed the woman; her sadness
unbruised and uninflamed.

As they laded her aboard
the ambulance, she slept.
Nearby, a fellow bellowed
and swore a blue streak,
"fokking fokk, kúkalabbi!
Someone hit my truck."

"Man, hold out your hand.
Don't be afraid. My little mink
will help you think straight."
The kind-mink wriggled
up his arm and the man
snuggled him into his chest.

He hesitated, anger flushing
his face, forehead unfurrowing
a tiny bit. The fine-mink rubbed
his back against the man's chin
and began to spin
into the man's hands.

The commotion slacked;
the man's heart braked;
his mood shifted from fifth
into neutral. His petrol cooled.
Despite his truck being battered,
the dent no longer mattered.

I know my purpose now:
deliver kindness to the angriest.
Seek them out in dirtiest pubs
and clubs, all over the island¬¬.
Appease the mountain dwellers.
Quell the berserkers.

Kakistocracy

*"Is ours a 'government of the people by the people for the people',
or a kakistocracy rather, for the benefit of knaves at the cost of fools?"*
                                            —Russell Lowell (1876)

Unqualified and unhinged, the worst governs:
climate denier, chronic liar, policy eradicator.
Unqualified and unhinged, the worst parents:
discipline denier, chronic liar, constant alienator.

Climate denier, chronic liar, policy eradicator,
each appointee finds utopia in creating dystopia.
Discipline denier, chronic liar, constant alienator,
each parent must value children over myopia.

Each appointee finds utopia in creating dystopia,
belittling fact or degrading church and state.
Each parent must value children over myopia
or revenge, instill compassion not boiling hate.

Belittling fact or degrading church and state
dismantles the warp and woof of government.
Revenge does not instill compassion but hate.
Work in tandem to restore and communicate.

Dismantling the warp and woof of government
will create chaos, distract us, install schemes.
Work in tandem to restore and communicate.
Kindness spoils disloyalty. Unity ruins regimes.

Aftermath

The trauma, ancient and antediluvian,
swept basalt lava out in a wide plain.

Hundreds of years passed but every day
lava flows from Seljalandsfoss to Brúarfoss:

newlyweds fight over finances, slam doors;
a woman vents at a child over nothing;

a driver erupts at a tourist for slowing;
a couple ruptures and releases cruel letters.

The accumulation of casualties posits untold
stone cairns, stacked and pointing south,

while the lava fields, jagged and honed
like filet knives, slowly become overgrown

by a thick mat of moss. It rounds the edges
and dulls the threat. When anger cools

and minds quiet, can we see the damage,
the catastrophic cost? People walk amongst

this atoll of rocks; comment on the ugly
toll of condemnation and isolation,

willows twisted and thrashed by nasty winds.

The Landscape

Early on, it seemed incomprehensible
Like distant mountain ranges
Or the infinity of oceans.

But as I reached the foothills,
I nearly touched your hand
And knew it possible.

From then on, I knew it was you
And I began in earnest
The arduous climb to you.

There were days in the lower
Reaches, where I felt my gear
Was wrong, not acclimating.

Once I hid in my tent deciding
To give up. But in the half-light
I realized I had the gall to do it.

I rose and tackled this snowfield,
Huge fissures of ice, crevasses
So wicked I held my breath

As I crossed old aluminum ladders.
I never gave up hope and pushed on
Through scree and boulder nightmares.

My knees and ankles nearly buckling
At every step. But up ahead, the beauty
Of the mountain shrouded in her secrecy.

I charged forward, bundled up
And ready for the worst storm
Of ever, brutal, apocryphal winds.

A rage I have never seen before,
Tearing out tent stakes, brandishing
Young hearts, trying to push me over.

But now the glacial bay is mine
And the clouds open wildly
And the climb is about consistency.

Haifoss

With gear and tripod, my hike was brutal:
cattle path, jostling people and crueler winds.
The children clamored up the stairs and squiggled,
then began the breakfast banter, resigned.

Cattle path, jostling people, crueler winds,
I chased the light, will it dull and fizzle?
They began the breakfast banter, resigned;
once angry children now seemed settled.

I chased the light but it did not dull or fizzle,
instead it refracted and intertwined.
Once angry children now seemed settled.
Good humor replaced the nasty or unkind.

Instead it refracted and intertwined
with the waterfall, bright and luminal.
Good humor replaced the nasty or unkind.
I tousled hair, both playful and delightful.

The Skáld and the Drukkin Tröllaukin
— *Told through 21 hattatals, Ancient Norse forms*

Hyrniardi
— *The Tröll's Verse*

Swollen & locked in this curse, stuck,
Swept & cajoled into a troll,
Bypassing crass laws, conviction,
Consequences never ever felt.
Required: reach for drink each day:
Rum, gin, Brennivin (with shark) or whiskey.
Dry drunk: erase dwarf, replace with man.
Dry drunk: feel the path of wrath, death.

Goldralag
— *Incantation Verse*

Tröllaukin dishonored the law.
Tröllaukin dishonored women's bodies.
Tröllaukin dishonored his family
To avoid prison,
To avoid penance
& his children's scorn.
The tröll shall accept this spell.
The tröll shall accept his shape.

Sextánmeter
— *Sixteen-Sentenced Verse*

Farmers grieved. Folks donated.
Followers prayed. All pitied.
Hoaxes jinxed. Sorcery jerry-rigged.
Judgment suspended. Lawyers fooled.
Stories spun. Naïve bamboozled.
Spinsters duped. Children hoodwinked.
Skáld queried. He questioned.
Queen scoffed. King rebuked.

Refhvörf
— *Antithetical Verse*

Haters love the human-tröll,
Halfway-whole? Smoothed splinters?
Sheepish wolf? Blood-lusting willows?
Where everything, nothing makes illogical sense.
Schemers strategize lust & common decency.
Schemers contemplate occasional loyalty.
Unread skáld bangs out valuable baubles,
Brand new wrecks, & manageable hurricanes.

Alhent
—Fully-Rhymed Verse

Skáld studied, scrawled, bloodied
Sanity, prosody, vanity, bourgeoisie,
Taught validation, sought vindication.
Venue disguised, ingénues queued.
Beauteous alhents, gorgeous áttmælts
Accentuating precision, anticipating revolution.
Backroom valiants consumed brilliant
Balladry, rapport, & espirit de corps.

Runhendur
—End-Rhymed Verse

Townswomen tacked eiderdown quilts,
Terrified ogress might raid, tilt
Axes, abduct all men, wilt
Ardor, induce personal guilt.
Avoid catastrophe, sally forth search,
Secure wagons, move church.
Drive ogress away, beyond birches,
Between deep spires, her new perch.

Thríhent
—Three-Part Rhyming Verse

The last tröll stole mesmeric men,
Mostly young, unsung, & strong.
Yearly, she picked & preyed,
Propelled, then repelled by bethel bells.
The new troll siphoned sloppily,
Sleeping deep on steep
Columnar cliffs, deadly drunk,
Daring, uncaring, barely conscious.

Langlokur
—Late Conclusion Verse

Everyone seems calloused, cracked—
Closed off from certainty, facts.
Artists shaped metal, languished strokes,
Sang churches from foundations.
Doubt wracked all my small ships,
Shattered ribs & seized bilges.
Scuppers plugged; pumps clogged-fouled.
—People care, are verse-listening.

Stamhendr
—*Stammering Verse*

Hammered, he found Fossarfoss,
Frolicked like three children,
Chased after crows. Crowberries
Comforted like warm skyr.
Townsfolk ridiculed (his) ridiculous,
Reinforced by verse, they tersely
Judged, knowing crime, criminal,
Curbed moral responsibility.

Áttmaelt
—Eight-Sentenced Verse

Knitters purled stitches like lines.
Laborers fixed fences like stanzas.
Herders sang poems to spring lambs.
Smiths rang songs to raging iron.
Laziness never righted the riggwelter.
Recent shornies must have summer.
Excessiveness winnows the weak.
Winter cattle need barriers from wind.

Ordskviduháttr
—Proverb Verse

One should not live only in the city.
Own actions. Meet for laughter.
Never flee behind masks or flasks.
Find secret waterfalls & discern.
Learn neighbors. Greet derelict dogs.
Do read others lives like long novels.
Don't hurry children. Have patience.
Help elders harvest without payment.

Skiálfthenda
—Shivering Verse

Sickened, townsfolk thought, acted,
"Take down tröll from his rock.
Make him face himself as a man.
He has disguised truth for too long."
Roped, anchored to barn, troll begged,
Begged for drink; they offered water.
Sobriety loomed, dropped like fog,
Lowering itself into the valley.

Dróttvaett
—Five-Syllables Staggered Verse

Twelve hours passed, no twists.
Tröll faded, man (David) emerged.
Loose ropes, loops grounded.
Lost in clothes, reduced.
Jury formed. Judge paced.
Jail. Conviction. Time.
Skáld saved. Felt valued.
Sensed validation.

Flagdaháttr
—Monster Verse

David muttered sorry. Mouthed
Mad apologies. Sad,
Bitter, depressed, did not
Discern badness, wrong turns.
Any antiphons fell flat,
Amends merely empty cups.
Children suborned, subverted.
Seen as means, mechanisms.

Stál
—Inlaid Verse

Now the country showed sense:
Skáld was fully enthralled,
Scrawled intimate inscriptions
Inside books, dignified.
Justified, truth triumphed,
Telling "No man is king."
Lava reshapes land, burns,
Lambastes hate & waste.

Dunhenda
—Echoing Rhyme Verse

Suddenly, skáld traveled away,
Strangers willing to pay.
Traversed three continents,
Tried to find contentment.
Crowds couldn't understand
Cursed trölls or reprimands.
Whispered "Why the repute?
Why the dogged pursuit?"

Tuískelft
—Double Shaken Verse

Deep & dank, the prison
Desolated David,
Turning (him) toward assent,
Torrid flows, volcanoes
Boiled whole bodies of lakes:
Baked new land, uncharted.
There, pink, tiny flowers
Thrived, a million bouquets.

Ridhendur
—Rocking Rhyme Verse

Skáld unknowingly steered
South, arrived at dungeon.
Guards vigorously guided:
Gruff, aggressive, hostile.
"Tröll, magnanimous Tröll,
Today I forgive all.
Hate, eviscerating hate
Hampered my happiness."

Togdrápulag
—Journey-Poem Meter Verse

"That tröll perished by
Truth. This man stands stripped,
Humbled by (your) hattatals &...
Honored by (your) devotion."
Skáld stepped back by then,
blinked, winced & winked.
"Acceptance proves people, through
prodding, can change, rearrange."

Formlaus
—Formless Verse

In ceaseless darkness, try
Not to doubt spring, nor
The Soul. Humans tend
Towards tröll. Light drives
Them out. Awfulness
Should be buried under-
Ground, left to nourish
Thrift & woolly willows.

Munnvörp
—Improvisation Verse

Oystercatchers nested,
Calmly doting on young.
Glacial rivers were milk,
Waterfalls open tongues.
People gathered onshore,
Careful with each other,
Loved & bonded well
Like clusters of campions.

The Mead of Poetry

Hidden in the Wilderness of Mirrors,
concocted with blood, honey and tears,

it was stored by dwarves in a hollow cave
in a barrel fitted with staves, then sealed

like a grave with dirt and prayed over
for no escape. And while volcanoes roared

and spewed, recovery seemed an impossibility.
No one would ever find the Mead of Poetry.

No one would ever versify like Dickinson,
Whitman, Plath or the Bard. Each sipped

hard at the elixir, yet no other voice would
drip with irony or ooze with silky syllables.

Squelched, the mead would waste away,
never seeing daylight or the Milky Way.

But there was a young poet, dead broke
and adventurous, who believed in its existence,

traveled half the globe to unearth its puissance.
On a hunch, he dug and found a trove of treasure.

He awkwardly pulled the firkin from the ground,
pried hobnail with hammer, unsealed and found

an ice-cold mead, a clear beer. Ladling a draw,
he poured a draft and drank it slowly and steadily.

Every sound from every language ever known
registered in his mind. Every word ever written

flew across his eyes. Monuments appeared last
and hovered on the horizon like bits of glass.

His whole being swam in poetic discourse,
a hurricane of phrases and diction. Then and only

then, each word clicked like a trigger; each line
juddered like cable to an elevator; each stanza

vibratoed like an orchestra. He wrote longhand
for three days straight, the most brilliant

verse ever composed. His poetry heaved:
glaciers skidding across alluvial plains,

an abstractionist painting murre eggs,
bodies of isolated prisoners aching for touch,

a blue fox's blending into highland hills,
the trapeze artist's release electrifying us all.

Kerið Crater

They observed from a safe
Distance, from stout horses,

From a mountain away, borne
By grief, designed by anger,

Three thousand years ago.
Magma gushed. Depression emptied.

Caldera formed. An eye socket.
An ear hole. A broken bowl.

Bits crumpled. Soil settled.
Seed fluttered. Rhizomes rooted.

Water pooled in a hand.
A serving dish glimmered.

Ground water percolated.
Aqua replaced red dust.

One blue eye. One flat ear.
A turquoise sequin. An end stop.

We climbed. We peered.
We wondered. We left.

The sun arcs back
Like an ancient pendulum.

The moon is opaque
Like the skin of an onion.

What was cruel is calming.
What was plain is beauty.

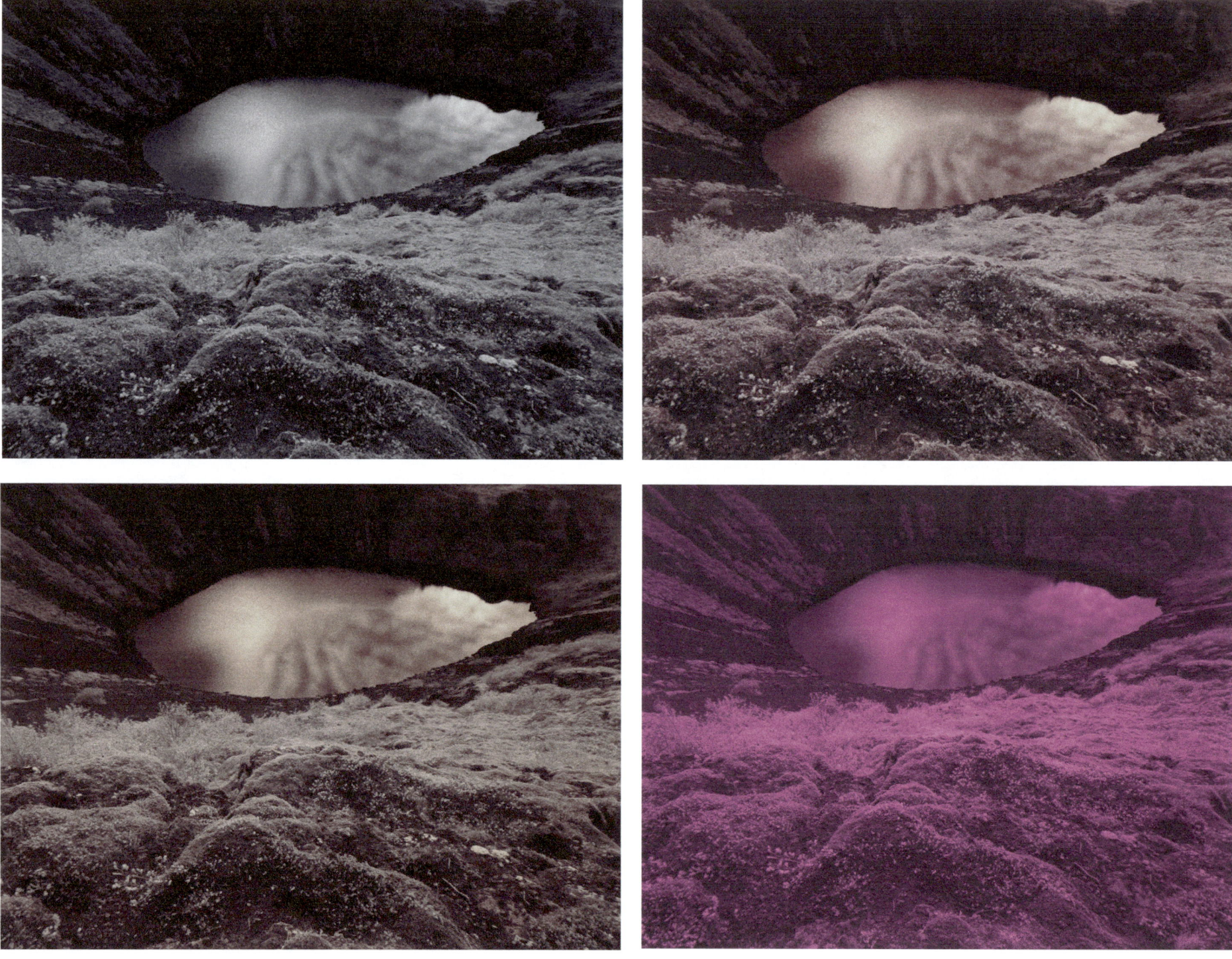

Six Angles of Puffins

I.
A spirited priest.
A foppish imp.
A clever mime.

An opera singer.
A scuba diver.
A faithful lover.

A friar.
A Scot.
A monk.

II.
Little Lutherans
gossip after church,
dressed in Sunday best.

Down in the cellar,
a child scuttles, peeking
through a doorway.

White-washed cemeteries,
steeples of stone lean
against a blue sea.

III.
Engorged cheek patches
are yellow and swirling
like brain coral.

Mouth a watery
bed of oranges
engraved for love.

Kelp-stained beaks
rouged brightly
for nodding displays.

IV.
Black shape, too large
for comfort, translucent
fish scales for eyes.

Two too narrow wings,
feathers like hooks
lift and float me in air.

Rejoin me to rock,
the sanctity of my wings,
circling the brood.

V.
Chainsaws in the fog
chased by bellows and grunts:
a comic intermezzo.

The beakful of sideways
capelin disappear into riprap,
delivered minutes fresh.

Repel downward,
skyward with grapnels.
A mischievous superhero.

VI.
Thousands fly
overhead and underseas.
They appease ritual.

Everything changes.
Curiosity kills.
The summer ends.

Survivors shed their labels,
blend into themselves
and wash the earth away.

Vermin

Discerned a blur near Reykjavik,
discovered a den outside Hornvik,

Turned out false, abandoned. Tried
conjuring one in winter, in fog, in rain.

Thought one sat on my door stone,
another one asleep on my sod roof.

Nothing. Dreams betokened, hopes
befouled, all lovers bemoaned.

It is all self-doubt, a curse of coastline,
an omen of open space. Every oblong

rock, every flash across the horizon
shudders me. Perhaps there was no

blue fox. It has angered too many
farmers, muzzled too many sheep,

gruesome suffocations gurgling blood.
It has destroyed too many eider nests,

protector passed out in early hours.
Prized for its bluish pelt, it was displayed

at waterfall giftshops and worn about
town. It was hated simply because it fits

the myth like a wolf and terrorizes
the countryside by killing everything so

they say. And then one day, there it was:
a tail like an immaculate scarf, coat

mottled and shedding winter, a noticeable
limp from a shotgun last fall, fur more

brown than blue, eyes inquisitive
and solemn, body smaller than I ever

imagined, lithe and deft along cliff
edges. This animal was my darkest

shadow, a visual reminder of all my losses.
Its ancestors were the original settlers,

navigated polar ice to homestead here.
I followed it down, crisscrossed paths,

and marveled as it snagged a puffin
in a single charge and mantled it,

killing it swiftly and humanely.
Away she went carrying her ornately-

wrapped package to her four pups.
And their joy of food. Their energy.

I laid on the hill and prayed aloud
for their safe keeping, for them

to survive against all the wrong
perceptions and diabolic myths

created by the fickle crowds.
I prayed for safe passage across

armlets of rivers and farmers'
pastures. I prayed for the sea to roll

in their dinner, molluscs and cod,
for the foxes to be well fortified

in the leanest times, for hunters'
rifles to be locked away in back

cupboards, uncleaned and unused.
For them to be vermin no more.

Svartifoss

This embodies blackness, the grimness
of complete darkness, the frozen drool

into a dead eye pool. Basalt columns sheer
topple, strength undermined by our faults.

Divorce is a solidified cataract, stuck,
stock-still in winter, desperate for spring,

for the warfare to end, for the children not
to testify, for the courts to render fairness.

The audience stands well clear of debris,
picks a spot and waits for the collapse.

The photographer renders his decision
based on logic, the right white balance.

In Iceland, the cold brutalizes the land,
cracks and chips at rock; instability reigns.

Luckily, I have carved a home into stable
sandstone and fashioned it with twin furnaces,

mine and hers. I hunker down for perpetual
dark, the pick axe assault on my bedrock.

Who knew cruelty came in so many forms.
Who knew a handwritten letter could press me

to weep for days or my daughter could disown
me and vow to never see me again. Who knew

my brothers would shun me, their shoulders
shrugging in no light. Who knew I would find

a woman, hot with lava and plumes of steam
who shifted my plate tectonics. Who knew

I would find a love, multilayered and replete
with fossils, a waterfall melted by our heat.

Myths and Rumors

Children, despite your unwillingness
to speak, listen to these stories.

Look out the truck window. Here,
in Dimmuborgir, those formations

look like hunched over figures.
It is written they are the bodies

of dwarves who partied until sun
baked their bodies into hardened

lava. Remember the tiny álfhóls
we saw along the road? Elves

visit in the night. Reynisdrangar's
coast looks like trolls locked in rock

as they attempted to steal ships
with ropes. Some trolls supposedly

steal bad people and children and eat
their hearts in dank caves. The giant

Lagarfljót worm undulates through
broken river ice searching for victims.

Remember when your father claimed
I took steroids when I competed

in a drug-free strongman and lifted
a car 24 times? Or when he claimed

I was gay and when he said I had
three girlfriends besides your mom?

Which seem fanciful, contradictory?
Which of these is provable and true?

Reversal of Misfortune

Frozen waterfalls become liquid, brown
grasses are as green as kelp. Impassible
roads become passable. Snow storms negligible.
No more chains for the four-wheel drive.

My ex-wife lets me see the dog every
weekend. She forgives my impetuousness,
my disloyalty. We become new friends
and I come over to clean her gutters.

My daughter calls me on the phone
and we connect about her new police
job, her Bernese, her anger. Her absence
no longer denies my fatherly existence.

My brothers sit with my poems, emotions
enveloping them like fog around Stokksnes,
unshrouding secrecy, revealing unsayable,
unimaginable binaries and privileges.

My wife's ex-husband enters rehab,
his liver and kidneys loaded with toxins.
We take the children full-time, recovery
uncovers more and they adjust medications.

My step-children now accept their father's
role, his brainwashing, his need to exact
revenge on their mother. They soften to us
like freshly-weaned puppies. Warm our arms.

The seismology needle quiets. All volcanoes
lie dormant. Geysers stop venting. Glaciers
begin growing. Hot springs cool. Fewer tourists
are able to visit. Our island becomes stable.

Smoldering

—Ekki er sopið kálið þótt í ausuna sé komið
There's many a slip between cup and lip.

Rust-orange and thin-skinned, the trawler,
long abandoned and beached, smoldered

like a dry cigarette in the heat, slowly
listing, inebriated, into gravel. Hull nearly

eaten clean by oxidants and sun, pockmarked
as if by aggressive cancer. Vulture gulls coated

the deck lab-coat white. The ship's nets thrown
to shore long ago to smother wildflowers or trip

locals. The captain was a semi-liquid vent,
vodka-soured and odium-fueled, hell bent

on controlling his crew. Drank at the wheel.
Fed the mariners rancid puffin and minke meat.

Braggadocious, he was the best captain ever,
no man was more seaworthy or clever.

"No, that captain don't pay twice as much. Swear.
Lies. Lies. His ship is puny, much smaller.

They don't admire him. His crew is cracked.
I call bullshit. His fishing nets rarely packed."

Woke them in the blackest black, from thin bunks
to slur orders, reinforce their idiocy, dead drunk.

After he passed out, they all snuck onto a dingy.
No wages, they said, are worth his rage. He's stingy

and crafty, crappy and filthy. They landed ashore
to walk home, happy to escape his boorishness,

surprised their wives as they slipped into bed, cold.
When the captain awoke, his ship was aground,

a hole in the bow, engine hissing, crew missing.
Taking the pistol out, he thought suicide, resisting,

fingering the trigger. "I've ruined the lives
of my crew, their families, my ex-wife,

her family, my friends. My beautiful
ship is fucked, stuck forever, its hull

cracked, nothing much here to salvage."
He lifted the bottle, studying the carnage,

climbed down, leaving the trawler to squat
in a wake of debris, diesel fuel and utter rot.

Visible Giants

I am struggling under the skull sky,
trying to identify what I see and feel.
They are not frost-ogres but veritable
loners, invisible giants are trailing me.

I need to help myself by helping others.

In the Southwest, Einangrast bathes
in the glacial rivers and golden waterfalls.
Only I see his form backlit from droplets
of mist and water, sixteen meters in height.

I photograph his shape to prove existence.

In the West, Úr is a vigilante, exiled sentry
over pufflings. He stands back of the cliffs
and herds the confused new ones into the sea.
Even though they try to comply, some fail.

I gather the stragglers and release to flight.

In the Northeast, Bömmer loves Sorg
but they are separated by curses and rivers.
He sleeps in a depression in the stone
forest, rocks echoing a melancholy melody.

I lift the curses by singing every Norse chant.

In the East, Sorg weeps in the only treed
forest; she has forgotten touch and her lover's
voice. I realize the shallowness of my own
hurt in her sorrow. No certainty of tomorrow.

I build four river bridges to connect the lovers.

The Shore of Corpses II
—a Ljodahattr, an ancient Norse form

Scorched and torched, all grass burned.
Possessions dropped. Parents carried
children. Children clung to parents. People
wept as they scurried to the cliff to escape
the doomsday of the gods. We all lined up
along the edge, cloistered and cornered.

We braced for a fiery grave, molten rock
tightening us into a fierce clump, the last
knot of humanity, our calamity almost over.
But the sea began to raise itself up, defying
gravity, flooding to our knees, neutralizing
the threat in great sheaves of steam and smoke.

Now, the great hall was ash; all the land-
murderers and oath-breakers are entombed
in rock casement in the basement of Niflheim.
Unsown fields blossom. Dry waterfalls
resume. Sheep refill the fields. There
is a resurgence in human decency.

Children scamper and play, unhampered
by countries or origins or prejudices. Theirs
is a scraped tablet, a tabula rasa. The world
merges to one continent, the greatest Pangea,
rejoined by catastrophe, by the lewd crowd:
amoral, baseless, clueless and infantile.

Baldr and Hod reconcile. Live in houses
next door. Tell stories of their misspent
youths, their father, their mother. But now
they are best friends instead of estranged
brothers. They fish the Greenland Sea
in a wooden boat they built together.

Children and step-children kneel
at the brothers' feet, soaking in the tales,
the new myths. They speak their own
stories of mending, of green beauty
sweeping across the island, of bounty,
of rebirth, of forgiveness and love.

Notes on Poems

Dóttir: daughter
Dreadnought: thick coat for stormy weather
Laikskáld: dramatic author
Laxganga: salmon entering the mouth of a river
Pyrrhic victory: victory where win is catastrophic to winning side
Redd: salmon nest in gravel
Samfell: collapse
Sálmur: canticles/hymns/poems
Semtex: plastic explosive containing RDX and PETN
Skáld: poet
Sótop: soot door
Steindur: cairn
Stö∂va: stop!
Vallholl: heaven but in form of a great hall

In Norse mythology, Baldr, the good, and Hod, the blind, reconcile their differences and live together. This is after the earth is cleansed of evil (Njar∂dvik 91). Niflheim is the dark-world, a cold hell (101). Ironically, I used to work in a building called Niflheim and it was cold in winter and hot in summer, perpetually.

Laufey was the mother of Loki and Loki's father was Farbauti (Dangerous-Striker). Loki is claimed to have gotten the good from Laufey and the bad from Farbauti (37). Urri∂afoss means "Trout Falls."

The mead of poetry is a myth that is strung through Norse myth. Any person who drinks of it will have extraordinary poetic powers (Lindow 224-227).

"Einangrun dregur bunglyndi oft á langinn" means "Isolation often perpetuates depression."

Einangrast means isolation in Icelandic. Úr means banishment in Icelandic. Bömmer means depression in Icelandic. Sorg means sadness in Icelandic.

Hatterals are spoken verse forms that come in 100 varieties. I selected 21 different ones to show the range of types and take on some of the harder forms. The most common is the Dróttvaett with its first syllable rhymes in lines one, three, five and seven, plus it has alliteration tracking from line one to two, from line three to four and so on. The majority of the forms follow alliteration patterns such as this; however, there are some distinctions to make between each form. For example, Sextánmaeltr has sixteen sentences built into eight lines of poetry. An Áttmaelt has eight sentences. One sentence for each line. A Stál inlays rhyme every other line, while a Langlokur has a late conclusion as it answers the first sentence. For the Refhvörf, words dissimiliar to each other are placed within lines. For example, I used "valuable baubbles," which is antithetical since baubbles are cheap. The Dunhenda uses end rhyme in each two lines (one and so on).

Ordskviduháttr is essentially writing in proverbs, while Tuískelft has alliteration in lines one, three, five and seven with a syllable between to make it double shaken. A Ridhendur features rocking rhyme in the second, fourth, sixth and eighth lines. The Flagdaháttr contains rhyme in the second, fourth, sixth and eighth lines but there must be a multisyllabic word used in each case. A Skiálfhendt has alliteration separated by one syllable and a full rhyme within the third and sixth lines.

The Thríhent has three rhymes situated in the first, third, fifth and seventh lines, while an Alhent is fullyrhymed with two pairs of rhymes in each line. This one proved challenging as the verse can become cliched with too many rhymes. Cleverly, the Stamhendr doubles up on words that are the same within lines one, three, five and seven. As an example, I used "crow" and followed that with "crowberries" thus it stammers. A Hyrniardi was the first poem that holds eight syllables per line and rhymes in the middle of lines. The Draughent utilizes seven syllables per line and follows the rules of Dróttvaett. Lastly the Runhendur is end rhymed throughout the poem, while the Goldralag is based on incantation verse (Sturluson 167-220).

Works Cited

Anderson, R.B. *Norse Mythology: The Religion of our Forefathers, Myths of the Eddas.* Boston: Longwood Press, 1977.

Kauffmann, Friedrich. *Northern Mythology.* London: Northwood Press, 1976.

Lindow, John. *Norse Mythology: A Guide to the Gods, Heroes, Rituals, and Beliefs.* Oxford: Oxford UP, 2001.

Mackenzie, Donald. *Teutonic Myth and Legend.* London: The Gresham Publishing Co., 1891.

Njarðvik, Njörðdur. *The World of the Viking Gods.* Reykjavik, Iceland: Iceland Review, 2002.

Sturluson, Snorri. *Edda.* London: Everyman, 1987.

Special Thanks

I want to thank the Residency Program at Gullkistan Laugarvatni, specifically Alda Sigurðardóttir for allowing me to spend such productive time in Iceland, as well as Linda Michel-Cassidy, Jacques and Mari Desruisseaux, and Rachel Haley Himmelheber for inspiring me. I appreciate Alda Sigurðardóttir's husband, Jón, for his help with pronounciations of the various hattatals.

Appreciate the assistance of Gold Wake Press and Kyle McCord for his work on the book. Many thanks to Heather Derr-Smith, Kerrin McCadden and Matthew Gellman for the blurbs. And thanks to Leilani Luker for proofing.

I dearly appreciate my wife, Melissa Brooke, for taking care of the house, children and puppies while I was gone. It was wonderful to have time to create and explore without worry.

www.ingramcontent.com/pod-product-compliance
Lightning Source LLC
Chambersburg PA
CBHW042107090526

44590CB00005B/132